AND WITH
Great Joy

Written by:

John Mudd

Copyright © 2023 John Mudd

All rights reserved.

No part of this publication may be reproduced, distributed, or transmitted in any form or by any means, including photocopying, recording, or other electronic or mechanical methods, without the prior written permission of the publisher, except in the case of brief quotations embodied in critical reviews and certain other noncommercial uses permitted by copyright law.

Table of Contents

CHAPTER 1 — 1
911 BUTTERNUT STREET

CHAPTER 2 — 8
NATIVITY, JOHN CARROLL SCHOOL, AND TAKOMA

CHAPTER 3 — 14
ST JEROME, RESURRECTION, MEXICO

CHAPTER 4 — 20
MOUNT SAINT MARY'S, MONSIGNOR SATTERFIELD, VATICAN II

CHAPTER 5 — 30
QUEEN OF PEACE

CHAPTER 6 — 39
THE OFFICE OF SOCIAL DEVELOPMENT

CHAPTER 7 — 45
ST. AUGUSTINE, THE GOSPEL CHOIR, IMPAC

CHAPTER 8 — 64
ARCHBISHOP CARROLL HIGH SCHOOL / FORT BELVOIR

CHAPTER 9 — 77
RETIREMENT

Acknowledgment

I would like to express my gratitude to those who have played a significant role in encouraging me to document my experiences within the priesthood. I extend my appreciation to my brother and his wife, Phil and Marion Mudd, who were the initial champions of this endeavor. When I initially broached the idea of recording my reflections, it wasn't because I believed myself to be of great importance. Yet, my brother assured me of my significance to our family and urged me to undertake this writing journey.

I also wish to acknowledge my sister and her husband, Hilda and Don Lazas. My sister has consistently reminded me of her enduring support and the role she played in my achievements from the very beginning. I am equally grateful to their spouses, whose love and encouragement sustained me during my teenage years, throughout my educational pursuits, and throughout my service as a priest.

Furthermore, I extend my thanks to my nieces and nephews and their families. Their presence and love have always encouraged me.

In addition, I want to recognize my priest friends: Mike Bryant, Dick Gardiner, Ray Kemp, Mike Kelley, Larry Frazier, Pat Devine, Dan Devore, Gene Brake, and Bill Montgomery. These are exceptional priests whose friendship and example serve as a continuous source of inspiration to me.

I also wish to pay tribute to Monsignors James Montgomery and Ralph Kuehner, both of whom have since passed away. These men served as mentors and guides throughout my journey, and I am profoundly grateful for their influence.

I want to acknowledge Claudia Thorne, a parishioner of St. Augustine and a dear friend, whose encouragement prompted me to commence this writing project. I am also thankful to the many parishioners and friends I've encountered along the way, each of whom has offered their support and motivation for me to preserve some of my memories in writing.

Dedication

In honor of Philip and Hilda Mudd, my parents who emigrated to America during the early decades of the 20th century, originating from England and Ireland, respectively. Their deep affection for one another and their unwavering devotion to our family serve as the bedrock upon which my calling and life as a priest have been built.

CHAPTER 1
911 BUTTERNUT STREET

"To love God, to do the will of God,

to work for the good of others,

All this, always, everywhere,

And with great joy."

(Journal of A Soul, John XXIII)

Early in my studies at Mount Saint Mary's Seminary I came upon a variation of the above quote in The Journal of a Soul, written by Pope John the XXIII when he was a young seminarian. I loved John XXIII and thought that I wanted to have that same attitude as a student and eventually as a priest. I wanted to do the will of God and I wanted to do it with great joy. To this day whenever I feel depressed or wonder if I'm doing the right thing I revert back to my mantra and remind myself that if I'm not finding joy then I need to rethink what I'm doing. When I was a young priest, I was complaining about something and an older seasoned priest told me, "John, you have to learn to enjoy what you have to do." That may have been the best advice I received in those early days of ministry, because again when I feel challenged or asked to do something I would not otherwise choose to do, I tell myself to make it enjoyable. Find the joy in what is being demanded of me.

I am John Mudd and this is the story of my life, faith, and my calling as a priest in the Catholic Church. It begins with my parents, Philip and Hilda Mudd, and our home at 911 Butternut Street in the Takoma neighborhood of Washington DC. My mother, Hilda O'Connor, and my father, Philip Mudd, both immigrants from Ireland and England, respectively, embarked on their journey to America in search of a better life in the early part of the 20th century. Their paths crossed, and love blossomed, leading to their marriage in 1932. I arrived as the unexpected third child in 1943, completing our family with my sister, Hilda, and my brother, Philip.

As with so many immigrants, my mother's journey to America was marked by resilience and determination. At the tender age of 17, she left Ireland with only two years of high school education. Tragedy struck when her father passed away, compelling my grandmother to bring her seven children to the United States for a fresh start. My mother was the second youngest, and this courageous move laid the foundation for our family's future in America.

On the other hand, my father arrived in America from England as a valet for a vacationing wealthy Englishman. After returning to England, he soon realized that America held the promise of a better future for him, and in 1924 he made the decision to move to America permanently. Working as a butler, he often collaborated with Irish household staff, including some of my aunts and uncles. My father was dating my mother's sister, Maude, until he met my mother. Soon after they were dating and were married in 1932, when he was 33 and she was 22.

I was born as the "unplanned" addition to our family in 1943. My sister and brother were considerably older than I, and my birth came as a surprise. My mother used to tell me that my father was angry when he found out they were pregnant with me, but once born, I became a favorite. I fondly recall my brother's story about how shortly after my birth, my mother took me to the Convent at Nativity Church and School to introduce me to the Franciscan nuns who taught at the Nativity Elementary School. One of the nuns, moved by some divine inspiration, brought my mother, my brother, and me, the tiny infant, to the chapel and placed me on the altar. There, she offered a prayer, entrusting my future to God's will. My brother remembers that she looked at my mother and brother and said, "He will be a priest." From that day forward everyone assumed I would be a priest.

Growing up in my childhood home, religion held a central place in our lives. Church was an essential part of our weekly routine, and we never missed attending Mass on Sundays or Holy Days. While my father was initially Anglican, he embraced my mother's Catholic faith when they married, a testament to their deep love and commitment to each other.

My parents were not perfect, for they were human, but they were undeniably good people who loved their children deeply. They provided us with strong moral values and a profound faith in a loving and benevolent God. Their example instilled in me the importance of kindness, compassion, and the understanding that love and faith could transcend any challenges we face.

Once, after my parents were arguing and I was very upset, my father said to me, "Johnny, I'm not perfect, but I love you, and I will never leave you. You won't have to come looking for me in a bar or find me with another woman; I'll always be here for you." At the time, I didn't fully comprehend the weight of his words. I thought, "You're my dad; you're supposed to be here for me. Why would you even say something like that?" But as I grew older and gained more understanding, I came to realize the depth of my father's pain and his desire to break the cycle that had haunted him throughout his own life.

My dad had experienced the profound pain of being abandoned by his own father at the tender age of 12. He never had the opportunity to reconcile with him or even see him again. The absence of his father must have left an indelible mark on his life, shaping his perspective on family, love, and commitment. At that moment, my father was not only expressing his love for me but also making a promise. He wanted me to know that he would never repeat the mistakes of his own father. He was determined to be a constant presence in my life, providing the love and support that he never had.

As a child, I may not have fully grasped the gravity of his words, but as I matured, I began to see the immense strength and courage it took for him to make such a commitment. My father's words became a cornerstone of our relationship, a reminder of his dedication and his relentless effort to be a better father than he had.

Looking back now, I am deeply moved by my father's vulnerability and honesty at that moment. He bared his soul to ensure that I never experienced the pain he endured. His words were a declaration of his love and a testament to his determination to break the cycle of abandonment.

As the years passed, my father remained true to his promise. He was there for me through every milestone, offering guidance, encouragement, and unwavering support. He became my rock, a source of strength and stability in my life.

Today, I cherish the relationship I had with my father. His actions and sacrifices have shown me the true meaning of family, love, and perseverance. I am grateful for the lessons he taught me through his own experience and the love he poured into our relationship. In many ways, his words have become a guiding light in my life, reminding me to be present, compassionate, and dedicated to those I love.

I am also grateful for my brother and sister, Philip, and Hilda, who being considerably older than me, took on roles beyond that of siblings; they became role models, mentors, and, in many ways, like additional parents during my formative years.

Hilda, being the eldest had a protective and caring nature. She took it upon herself to guide me through the challenges of childhood and adolescence. Her wisdom and example were invaluable, as I observed her managing her teen and young adult years. She had many friends, from her Catholic school experiences but also from the neighborhood. I remember that she deliberately joined a sorority at our local public high school so that she would have a less narrow circle of friends and experiences. Her nurturing nature made her an excellent source of comfort and encouragement helping me navigate the ups and downs of growing up. Once when as a teenager I cut my lip playing basketball and required 13 stitches on the inside of my cheek, she asked me if I wanted to go to the movie. I learned then that the power of love can even soothe physical pain. Sitting next to my young adult sister at the movie was one of the happiest memories of my childhood.

Philip, my older brother, played a crucial role in shaping my character, values, and religious faith, as well as teaching me the fundamentals of football, baseball (basketball, not so much), swimming, and riding a bicycle. He even helped me learn Latin so that I could be an altar server at Nativity Church. Watching my brother and sister living their lives, practicing their religion, and becoming adults helped me along my path to maturity.

Both Hilda (we call her Honey in our family) and Phil served as remarkable examples of parenting and grandparenting as they built their own families. Witnessing their love, dedication, and nurturing approach to their own children and grandchildren inspired me and continues to inspire me to embrace the same values in my own life and ministry. Their commitment to raising their families with love and respect further solidified the importance of family bonds in my life.

As we all grew older together, I saw how Honey and Phil and their spouses faced their challenges with dignity and unwavering faith. They navigated difficult times with grace, leaning on their faith to find strength and hope. Their resilience in the face of adversity continues to inspire me.

Throughout my upbringing, I witnessed the power of faith and the positive impact it had on our lives as a family. The seeds of the prayer spoken over me by the caring nun at the altar would eventually sprout, guiding me toward my life's calling to serve as a priest.

As I reflect on my journey, I am filled with gratitude for the love and faith bestowed upon me by my parents. Their unwavering support and the strong foundation they provided nurtured my passion for the priesthood and my commitment to serving others. Their legacy lives on in my work, as I strive to follow the example they set for me, spreading love, compassion, and faith to all those I encounter in my ministry.

CHAPTER 2
NATIVITY, JOHN CARROLL SCHOOL, AND TAKOMA

"Trust in the Lord with all your heart ….

In all your ways be mindful of Him

And He will make straight your path."

(Proverbs 3)

Growing up, my elementary and high schools, along with my neighborhood, played a huge role in shaping who I am today. I started off attending Takoma Elementary School for Kindergarten. But then, my mom decided to enroll me in Nativity Elementary School, where my sister and brother had already gone. My father had a tough upbringing in England and was hesitant to spend money on private Catholic education. He thought public schools were good enough. He believed that getting a job and working hard was more important than formal education. However, my mom saw the value of Catholic education, and she was willing to take on odd jobs to cover the costs, which weren't too high in those days since the nuns and priests who staffed Catholic schools worked for stipends.

Nativity School became the center of our family life, and it was here that my siblings and I received a solid education and were formed in our faith and moral values. I made lifelong friends, and our family friends became like extended family. If we had a new friend, they'd have to pass the test at Sunday dinner where my parents would observe their table manners and behavior. Once approved, they were always welcome in our home.

I have vivid memories of my early school years. In first grade, we had 100 students split into two sessions: 50 in the morning and 50 in the afternoon. Second grade was memorable because it was the year I made my first Confession and received my First Holy Communion. I loved my first and second-grade nuns.

In the third grade, I learned to read. I became fascinated with comic books and decided to learn to read the words in the comic bubbles. So, I set my mind to it, and soon enough, I was reading.

The next four years of elementary school passed in a blur. I was an average student and quite immature for my age. To cover up my insecurities, I often goofed around and didn't take my studies seriously. In eighth grade, my teacher compared me to my sister, who was bright, polite, and disciplined. She told me, "You are nothing like your sister." I'm not sure if it boosted or shattered my self-esteem, but I did think, "At least you didn't have to deal with my brother; he would have tested your patience!"

Nativity School and Church left a lasting impact on my spiritual and personal growth. I will forever be grateful for the education and values I received there. I made good friends at Nativity, many of whom I am still in touch with. Two of my best friends were Freddie Toibero and Frank

Davis. I remember Frank from 2nd grade onward, and Freddie I met in 8th grade. The three of us hung around a lot together in our high school years. My parents were very supportive of our friendships.

After Nativity School, it was time for high school. I had initially planned to follow in my brother's footsteps and attend St. John's Military High School and College. However, I ended up on a waiting list for St. John's so I enrolled at Archbishop Carroll High School instead. I didn't want to wear a military uniform, and Carroll was the first fully integrated secondary school in Washington, D.C. I felt drawn to be part of that experiment in integrated education, and in retrospect, I believe the Holy Spirit guided me toward my future in ministry.

Carroll High School turned out to be the right place for me. On the very first day, I made friends who are still dear to me today. Little did I know that two of my classmates, who introduced themselves to me on that day, would later become two of the school's most generous supporters. Another classmate I met the first day in my first class went on to become a fellow priest.

Although I wasn't an outstanding student at Carroll, I loved the school and cherished the friends I made there. The Augustinian priests who taught and ran the school were exceptional educators. Some of them took me under their wing and helped me discover my talents and purpose in life. While they were tough and demanding, I never felt mistreated. Whenever I got into trouble, I knew I deserved it.

High school was also the first time I had interactions with Black students. Although D.C. was segregated at the time, Carroll was an integrated school. While there was still de facto segregation in every aspect of our lives outside of school, Carroll helped me to appreciate we were all the same in the eyes of God.

Initially, like many White people in that era, I held certain prejudices and biases, but my time at Carroll changed my perspective significantly. Interacting with my Black peers taught me that we were all the same, with equal intelligence and talents. In fact, I discovered that some of my Black classmates were even more gifted than the White students. It was a valuable lesson that began to open my eyes to the racism that was endemic to our American society.

As I grew older, I came to realize that while I perceived the school as integrated, the Black students experienced it differently. They had to make significant sacrifices, leaving behind their friends, schools, neighborhoods, and even their culture to attend a predominantly White high school with an entirely White administration and teaching faculty. They faced the reality of racism every day, even though many of us White students were oblivious to their struggles. In later years, when I had the honor of presiding at a funeral for one of my Black classmates, I referred to our integrated high school in my remarks. However, another classmate spoke up and corrected me, emphasizing that he had attended a White school. It was a poignant reminder that the experience of integration was drastically different for Black students, and they faced significant challenges as pioneers of change in our racist society. My time at Carroll was a powerful awakening to the racism that persisted in our American culture, and it deepened my commitment to promoting equality and justice throughout my life.

Besides my school life, I also had many friends in my Takoma, D.C. neighborhood. I spent a lot of time at the Takoma Playground and Swimming Pool, where my love for sports grew. I wasn't the best player, but I loved the games, the camaraderie, and learning about different sports. Coaching little kids in football and baseball gave me confidence in myself.

During my sophomore year at Carroll, I wanted to play football, but I was too small for the high school team. Instead, I joined the Police Boys Club team in my neighborhood, where kids played in their own weight classes. However, that year, the Police Boys Club was forced to integrate. We had practiced for three weeks and were about to play our first game when the coach announced that rather than integrate the Police Boys Club would not have a football season. Again, racism and segregation were prevalent in our Metropolitan DC community. I found another league in Montgomery County Maryland and signed up to play for the Silver Spring Boys Club and enjoyed playing throughout my high school years.

High school was also when I started to consider my vocation. The priests at my parish and school had always earned my respect, and one day, I went to my parish priest to express my interest in becoming a priest. He advised me to read the Bible and we would discuss it later. Although the Bible initially bored me, I found inspiration in the book of

Proverbs and found in Proverbs 3:5-6 a guiding message throughout high school and beyond: "Trust in the Lord with all your heart... and He will make straight your path." I was attracted to girls in those years, and I dated a few times, but more and more I knew I wanted to be a priest.

As high school graduation approached, my mentor, Father Jim Montgomery, encouraged me to attend a regular college before entering the seminary. I settled on attending St. Francis in Loretto, Pennsylvania, but the tuition was beyond my family's means. Father Montgomery suggested St. Jerome's College in Canada, where the tuition was more affordable, and the pre-theology and Latin curriculum was ideal for my aspirations. It helped that the Catholic Archdiocese of Washington was willing to loan me the tuition, room, and board costs, with the proviso that if I went on to the priesthood, I would only have to pay back half the loan. The decision to attend Saint Jerome College set the course for my future in ministry.

In 1961, after graduating from John Carroll, I embarked on a new journey to St. Jerome's College in Kitchener, Ontario, Canada, excited about what the future held for me.

CHAPTER 3
ST JEROME, RESURRECTION, MEXICO

"The joys and the hopes, the griefs and the anxieties of the men of this age,

especially those who are poor or in any way afflicted, these are the joys and hopes,

the griefs and anxieties of the followers of Christ."

(Gaudium et Spes, 1965)

In the fall of 1961, I began my journey at St. Jerome's College in Canada, an experience that would profoundly impact my life. The college drew students from different states in the United States and various provinces in Canada, creating a diverse community of like-minded individuals with strong Catholic backgrounds.

The faculty, composed of priests from the Congregation of the Resurrection, played a vital role in shaping our intellectual and spiritual growth. Their guidance challenged us to become better versions of ourselves, fostering a love for learning and faith. The curriculum, which placed a strong emphasis on Thomistic philosophy and Latin, demanded a high level of rigor. Proficiency in Latin was considered indispensable for engaging in Catholic worship and comprehending Church documents. Additionally, depending on the specific major seminary, a significant number of theology courses continued to be taught in Latin.

Living with roommates for the first time taught me valuable lessons in cooperation and understanding, strengthening the bonds we formed. Engaging in extracurricular activities, such as intramural sports, kept us active and healthy.

After our first year, St. Jerome's College moved to the University of Waterloo, marking a new chapter in our journey. The transition brought a clear separation between the "non-clerical" students and those of us destined for ordination. At the renamed Resurrection College, the atmosphere became more seminary-like, focusing on comprehensive preparation for major seminary and a deeper study of philosophy. This marked a turning point for me and my fellow clerical students, as our dedication to the path of priesthood intensified.

As students at Resurrection College Seminary, we embraced a more rigorous preparation for our future responsibilities. Our appearance changed as we adopted cassocks, symbolizing our commitment to the priesthood and reminding us of the noble journey we were undertaking. Amidst the disciplined environment and rigorous curriculum, the camaraderie of my fellow seminarians provided comfort and support. Lifelong friendships were forged during those years, even as our paths diverged after graduation.

Living on the seminary campus fostered a strong sense of community, with like-minded individuals inspiring each other's dedication to their chosen vocation. The collective sense of purpose and shared values created an environment of mutual support and encouragement.

Throughout my time at Resurrection College Seminary, experienced priests mentored and guided us, enriching our spiritual formation and preparing us for the responsibilities of the priesthood. Their wisdom and insights were invaluable gifts as we embarked on this sacred journey.

During my academic journey, a unique opportunity arose as I was asked to chair the mission committee of the student government. Our mission was to promote the missionary activities of the Catholic Church and inspire our fellow students to appreciate the rich missionary history of our Church. Under the guidance of Father James O'Connor, who had a deep desire to serve in the missions himself, we worked diligently to encourage our peers to support and engage in these important efforts.

One significant event during my time at Resurrection College was the visit of a young man from St. Michael's College, Toronto, who introduced us to the CIASP, a program designed by the Maryknoll Society of the United States. This Conference for Inter-American Student Projects was created as a follow-up to Pope John XXIII's call for the First World to be more engaged in the developing world. CIASP allowed Canadian students to spend their summers participating in mission work, supporting Mexican clergy and communities in need. The presentation left a lasting impact on us, and a group of about seven or eight students from Resurrection expressed their interest in participating.

As chair of the mission committee, I took on the responsibility of coordinating their training, preparation, funding, and transportation for the CIASP project. The summers spent in Mexico were transformative and eye-opening. Although the conditions were challenging and the regions were impoverished, the experience brought us closer to the beautiful Mexican culture and its people filled with faith, hope, and love. I spent two summers in Mexico and in the process met and bonded with students from other Catholic colleges across southern Ontario, some seminarians, and mostly non-seminarian, male and female. To this day some of my closest friends are people I traveled on missions with to Mexico.

While many of us chose paths beyond the priesthood, our time at St. Jerome / Resurrection had a profound influence on our lives. The values instilled in us, the faith that was nurtured, and the friendships forged endured through the years. We continued to meet regularly for reunions, cherishing the memories and the shared purpose that had united us.

Looking back, I am grateful for the experiences, challenges, and friendships that blossomed during my time at St. Jerome's College and Resurrection. They prepared me for my life's work, instilled a deep sense of justice, and inspired a commitment to creating a more equitable and compassionate world. The impact of those formative years remains with me to this day, guiding me in my journey of life.

During our years together at St. Jerome / Resurrection in Canada, a momentous development was unfolding in the Catholic Church that would profoundly impact our lives and the future of Catholicism. In 1958, the same year we began our high school studies, Pope John XXIII, born Angelo Giuseppe Roncalli, was elected as the 261st Pope of the Roman Catholic Church.

Under Pope John XXIII's leadership, the Second Vatican Council, commonly known as Vatican II, was initiated in October 1962. This historic ecumenical council aimed to address the changing world and redefine the Church's role in it. The council was a pivotal turning point that challenged the traditional paradigm of the Church, urging it to engage with the modern world and advocate for social justice and peace.

As we immersed in our studies of philosophy and Latin, and grew in our spiritual lives, Vatican II was reshaping the Church's approach to spirituality, liturgy, and community engagement. We had been experiencing a religious and seminary life deeply rooted in Thomistic philosophy, centered around Latin studies, and a personal relationship with God – a "me and God spirituality." Vatican II, however, presented a new direction, calling for a more inclusive participatory, and ecumenical approach to faith, where the Church's teachings could resonate with people from all walks of life.

The Council encouraged Catholics worldwide to actively address social inequalities and promote a more equitable sharing of wealth and resources. Pope John XXIII's two major encyclicals, Mater et Magistra and Pacem in Terris, set the tone for Catholic engagement in the world, emphasizing the importance of justice, human rights, and peace.

One of the most significant developments during Vatican II was the Declaration on the Liturgy, which revolutionized Catholic liturgies, including the use of vernacular languages. This marked a profound shift in how Catholics experienced and participated in the sacraments and rituals, making them more accessible and relatable to the faithful.

As I reflect on my time at St. Jerome / Resurrection, I can now appreciate how the Catholic Church was being transformed without our awareness. The changes brought about by Vatican II were breaking down barriers of isolation and calling Catholics to be agents of positive change in the world. The Church was evolving to meet the challenges of a rapidly changing world, an evolution that continues to resonate with Catholics to this day, or at least those who experienced and still have the vision of Pope John XXIII and the Second Vatican Council.

CHAPTER 4
MOUNT SAINT MARY'S, MONSIGNOR SATTERFIELD, VATICAN II

"He who passively accepts evil is as much involved in it as he who helps perpetrate it. He who accepts evil without protesting against it is really cooperating with it."

(Dr. Martin Luther King)

Two eye-opening summers on a mission in rural regions of Mexico, witnessing the harsh reality of poverty faced by local communities left a lasting impact on my soul. Little did I know that this experience would profoundly shape my future, leading me to dedicate my life to a ministry focused on human and civil rights in the United States.

Upon my return, I found my country amidst the civil rights movement, with the voices of prophetic civil rights leaders like Dr. Martin Luther King Jr. resonating deeply within me. Their call for justice, equality, and an end to discrimination stirred a sense of responsibility to contribute to the struggle for a fairer and more just society. Although I had considered a life in social development and mission work abroad, I began to realize that my calling was to make a difference in my own country. While still aspiring to be a priest, I discovered a desire to serve in a non-traditional parish setting.

With my transformative Mexico experience and a new perspective on the world and the Church, I commenced my theological studies at Mount Saint Mary's Seminary in Emmitsburg, Md. in the fall of 1965. Some of my friends from Resurrection pursued studies at other major seminaries or chose different paths, including marriage and family life. A few Resurrection classmates joined me at the Mount. Having completed Latin and philosophy studies, we embarked on serious courses in Catholic theology and sacred scripture. The first year of theology proved academically challenging, but the discipline of regular prayer, meditation, and learning at Resurrection College prepared me. The campus at Mount Saint Mary's was notably larger, with a large lay student population. While we lived in a separate building and had separate dining halls, we interacted at athletic events, the library, and the student lounge. It was interesting being on a larger campus and closer to my home in Washington DC. I particularly enjoyed attending the Mount basketball games. The team was exceptionally good in those days and all the games were filled with excitement. It was a great diversion from the rigor of theological studies.

In the years between 1963 and 1965 four major decrees of the Second Vatican Council were promulgated:

1. The Constitution on Sacred Liturgy in 1963 which aimed to reform and renew the liturgy of the Catholic Church.
2. The Constitution on the Church in 1964 focused on the nature and role of the Church within the modern world.

3. The Constitution on Revelation in 1965 addressed the relationship between Scripture, Tradition, and the teaching authority of the Church.
4. The Pastoral Constitution on the Church in the Modern World in 1965 which explored the Church's stance on various social and ethical issues and its role in the contemporary world.

Unfortunately, both Resurrection College and Mount Saint Mary's Seminary, with a few exceptions, found themselves unprepared for the revolutionary concepts and direction that emerged from these documents and the Second Vatican Council (Vat II). The administration and faculty at these institutions were predominantly trained and steeped in an old paradigm of Catholicism and consequently struggled to fully embrace the transformative changes Vat II advocated.

The Council's groundbreaking teachings aimed to open Catholics to an entirely new way of being Church, fostering a more inclusive and dynamic approach to faith and spirituality. The lack of readiness in our seminaries hindered the smooth assimilation of these progressive ideas. The same could be said for the leadership in our Catholic dioceses and parishes. The Church was not prepared for the revolutionary changes that were in store, and perhaps because we were not prepared, we are still 58 years after the close of Vat II struggling as a Church to implement the vision of the participants in the Council.

With that proviso, I began my theological studies with enthusiasm, as did my fellow seminarians at the Mount. We did have one introductory course in theology, taught by a brilliant young professor, Fr. Jim Mulligan, on Revelation and he used the Constitution on Revelation as the basis of his curriculum. I remember it being the most difficult course I had ever taken up to that point, but it was also the beginning of my appreciation of what was to come in my education and later as a priest.

My second year at Mount Saint Mary's was perhaps the most exciting of any academic experience I had ever had. Monsignor Carroll Satterfield came to teach us systematic theology. In the context of a Catholic seminary systematic theology courses are an essential part of the curriculum and cover subjects such as Christology (the nature and role of Jesus Christ), Ecclesiology (study of the Church), Sacramental theology (study of the sacraments), Mariology (role of Mary), Eschatology (study of death, judgment, afterlife), and Moral theology (study of ethical principles and moral teachings).

With the exception of Moral theology, Monsignor taught all the systematic theology courses over a three-year period. I and most of my fellow seminarians will agree that Carroll Satterfield opened our minds to a whole new world of learning and theology.

Every course and every topic were examined comprehensively, beginning from the foundation in scripture through the history of the Church, looking at what every major theologian, both Catholic and Protestant taught and believed. It was a whirlwind of reading, studying, and learning. More than studying and learning, however, we were beginning to understand that there were various and sound ways of examining our faith and religion outside of the traditional study and defense of Catholic dogmas and doctrines, using syllogistic arguments and relying on manuals such as the Summa Theologica by Thomas Aquinas.

I am so grateful to Monsignor Satterfield for his approach to theology. He changed my way of studying and appreciating my faith. Of all my teachers at Resurrection and Mount St. Mary's, I dare say he understood what Vat II meant for the future of the Church.

Our Moral Theology left much to be desired. The professor was a good man, but very much rooted in old concepts and approaches. Prior to Vat II moral theology was dominated with an obsession with sin and condemnations of false teachings. Shortly prior to Vat II new approaches were being advanced with emphasis on dialogue, spiritual discernment, moral freedom, and the role of conscience. Our moral theology at Mount Saint Mary's was taught by one professor over a period of three years. He was old school and used old moral manuals. Once during my first course in moral theology, I asked a question related to a concept called "occult compensation." This notion pertains to clandestinely appropriating what is justly owed by another party who refuses to fulfill their obligation. In practical terms, it implies that under certain circumstances, taking from an employer who fails to provide fair wages could be morally justifiable. I recall a time when as a teenager I questioned my mother about my father potentially stealing ballpoint pens from his workplace. Her pragmatic response was, "John, your father isn't receiving proper compensation for his work, so if he occasionally takes pens for gifting or personal use, it's not the same as stealing." Though not formally acquainted with the concept, my mother was instinctively applying the principle of occult compensation.

As I was beginning my courses in moral theology in 1966 the United States was in the midst of the civil rights movement and there were demonstrations, sit-ins, and marches throughout the country as Black people were advocating for and demanding their rights. Amid demonstrations, instances of violence and looting were becoming more widespread. Becoming more sensitive to Black concerns I asked in the moral theology class whether looting could be rationalized using the principle of "occult compensation." My thinking was that Black people were only taking from businesses and institutions that had historically exploited them, thus seeking reparation for years of injustice. The professor lost his composure and started yelling at me, "What are you talking about? We are not talking about riots and looting. We are talking about justice!" After class that day one of the older seminarians, someone who had the same professor the year prior ran up to me and said, "John, we don't ask questions in the class." So, for the next three years, neither I nor anyone else ever asked a question in the moral theology classes.

Meanwhile, the United States grappled with a series of challenges including political assassinations, the civil rights movement, the Vietnam War, poverty and inequality, a profound shift in moral and sexual ethics, the arms race, and numerous other societal issues. And we went merrily along studying moral theology, largely detached from contemporary moral events and concerns.

Many of us were on our own engaging with moral theologians who exhibited a greater sense of enlightenment and responsiveness to modern concerns. We were into the documents emerging from the Vatican Council, which broadened our perspectives on concepts like dialogue, individual conscience, societal evil, human and civil rights, and social justice. During this time, I found my moral compass and conscience evolving in a different direction compared to the teachings presented in our moral theology classes. I began to cultivate an appreciation for the profound legacy of Catholic social teaching, as transmitted through social encyclicals such as Rerum Novarum, Quadragessimo Anno, Mater at Magistra, Pacem in Terris, and the then contemporary encyclical "Populorum Progressio" by Pope Paul VI.

With other classmates I read what other prominent moral theologians were writing and teaching at the time: I and my classmates were reading outside the class some of the current and great moral theologians of the day, such as Bernard Haring, Joseph Fuchs, and Charles Curran. They were associated with a "new moral theology" movement which emphasized a more personalistic and pastoral approach to moral issues. They were focused on moral principles and real-life situations, and they played a key role in shaping Catholic moral theology in the post-Vatican II era.

During my major seminary years at Mount Saint Mary, I particularly enjoyed the study of sacred scripture. We were introduced to a modern critical understanding of biblical interpretation which involved applying a range of scholarly methods to analyze and understand the Bible with its historical, cultural, literary, and theological contexts. This approach acknowledges that the Bible is a complex collection, library if you will, of books and texts written by different authors over centuries, and it seeks to uncover the intended meanings of these scriptures while understanding the layers of interpretation they may hold. This way of understanding scripture made perfect sense and enabled me to embrace modern science while at the same time holding fast to the principles of my faith. To this day with all the insights we have gained from the Hubble and Webb telescopes into the beginning of the universe, I see no contradiction with the Biblical stories or texts on which my faith is based.

My father continued to play a key role in my education and my priesthood. As an office supply salesman, one of his regular customers was The Liturgical Conference with an office in Washington. My father would visit there regularly and always come away with a handful of documents, pamphlets, and essays on the liturgical renewal which he in turn would mail to me. I was devouring everything the creative minds in the liturgical renewal were writing. One person in particular had a tremendous influence on my future and that was Fr. Bob Hovda. Hovda emphasized the need for liturgy to reflect the cultural and social context in which it is celebrated. He advocated for liturgical practices that engage with the everyday lives of people and address contemporary issues. With other leaders in the liturgical renewal, Hovda emphasized that liturgy should empower and involve all members of the Church in worship and mission. He connected the liturgy with social justice concerns, emphasizing that the liturgy should inspire believers to work for a more just and compassionate society.

Unbeknownst to my father at the time, his visits to the Liturgical Conference office and his sending me a wealth of the most innovative and creative insights emerging from the discussions surrounding the renewal of Catholic worship were forming me in the liturgical renewal. These were the ideas of some of the most creative minds of the era and they were shaping my understanding of prayer and worship and would later have an impact on my ministry at my first parish, Our Lady Queen of Peace, and later when I was pastor at Saint Augustine. By coincidence, years after my ordination, Fr. Bob Hovda attended a Mass at Saint Augustine at which I presided. The Mass was packed, the Gospel Choir had raised the roof, and the people were ecstatic with songs of praise, our parishioners were actively engaged as readers, eucharistic ministers, servers, and ushers, and I'm sure my message had something to do with social justice. After the Mass Hovda came up to me and said, "John, that was great; you are doing everything right at worship. My only suggestion is you should use real bread for communion." I could not have been more elated at the compliment.

As at St. Jerome's and Resurrection, I made lasting friendships at Mount Saint Mary's Seminary. My four years there paved the way for my life as a priest and my lifelong desire to continue to read and study scripture, and theology, and promote the renewal of Catholic worship.

CHAPTER 5
QUEEN OF PEACE

"In the restoration and promotion of the sacred liturgy the full and active participation by all the people is the aim to be considered above all else."

(Sacrosanctum Concilium 1963)

No doubt the Holy Spirit was guiding the process and after my ordination in 1969 I was assigned to a dynamic Black Catholic church in southeast Washington, DC. Stepping into this vibrant community, I was immediately enveloped by a sense of love and enlightenment. The people I met were faith-filled and passionate about their Catholic beliefs, but what struck me the most was their unyielding determination to challenge injustice both within the Church and society.

"I was woke," as they say, by the love and example of these remarkable individuals. They practiced their Catholic faith not only within the walls of the church but also by actively engaging in the fight for civil rights in their workplaces, neighborhoods, institutions, and even their Catholic Church. Their dedication to addressing social inequalities and systemic oppression was awe-inspiring and profoundly impactful.

My first Saturday hearing confessions at Queen of Peace was a memorable experience. As I entered the confessional,

I noticed a large poster of Pope Paul VI, who had recently issued Humane Vitae, reaffirming the Church's teaching on contraception. It was a time of significant debate and discussion within the Catholic community, and the parishioners at Queen of Peace were grappling with these teachings. The sisters who taught in the school put up the poster as a joke to remind me of the official teaching of the Church related to birth control and contraception. I soon understood, however, that the worst sins were not committed by two loving spouses but by the larger racist society of which the Catholic Church was a major offender. I realized that social sin and injustice were far greater offenses than anything loving spouses decided as they tried to create and raise their families.

Before joining Queen of Peace, I had known of the parish because of my time as a CYO football player. I remember playing against Queen of Peace, an all-White team in 1957. However, when I arrived in 1969, the parish and school had undergone a dramatic transformation, and it was now predominantly a Black community. The neighborhood had changed, and the parish had adapted to serve the new demographic.

My initial impressions of Queen of Peace were awe-inspiring. The church was packed every Sunday for three Masses, and buses were sent to various neighborhoods, including public housing sections, to pick up parishioners. The music and singing during Mass were exceptional, with congregational singing, even in harmony, creating a beautiful and uplifting worship experience. The priests who worked at Queen of Peace prior to my coming had trained the congregation in what Vatican II mandated: "the full and active participation of all the people" in the liturgy.

The parish had a vibrant community of priests, with four living in the rectory, three of us serving full-time. The school was bustling, and every child was Catholic, with two classes for each grade. The Daughters of Charity staffed the school, with only two lay teachers. Msgr. Charles Cremona, the pastor, ran a tight ship, taking an active role in the parish's activities and initiatives. He and I often butted heads. He was old school when it came to theology and liturgy, and I was a "new breed," as they called my generation of young priests. In retrospect, however, I respect Monsignor Cremona for his genuine love for his parishioners, his straightforward style of leadership, and his management of the school and parish. He would listen to new ideas and eventually support the Vatican II vision of the Church. During my time at Queen of Peace, we transitioned from Latin to vernacular worship and implemented the renewal of the celebration of all the Sacraments of the Church.

The athletic teams at Queen of Peace were exceptional, representing the parish with pride and talent. One standout memory was organizing a trip to Hershey Park for 13 buses filled with teenagers. Hershey Park is an amusement 124 miles distant from Washington DC. When we returned to the parish early evening, I was confronted by Mrs. June Harrison who asked me where her son, Keith was. I replied, "Isn't he on the bus?" She said, "No, Father. You left him in Hershey Park!" Years later I met Mrs. Harrison after a graduation ceremony for Archbishop Carroll High School. She asked me if I remembered her and I said, "Mrs. Harrison, there is no way on God's green earth, that I would ever forget you," and I inquired about Keith. She said he's doing well; he's an attorney in Michigan.

Queen of Peace had a strong emphasis on community and social programs. The Christmas scene that one of our parishioners, an art teacher in public school, created was a symbol of Christ's birth in the heart of our southeast neighborhood, bringing joy and hope to all. As I immersed myself in the community and witnessed the dedication of the people, I felt a profound sense of gratitude and a conviction that I was meant to be a priest.

The parish was actively engaged in tithing, and the parish council and CYO Council were active in making decisions and shaping the community's future. Queen of Peace was teeming with social programs for children, demonstrating the parish's commitment to supporting and uplifting the younger generation.

Father Richard Gardiner was the other young assistant priest at the parish. He was only a year older than I, but he brought a maturity to ministry that I didn't quite have. I was more impetuous and would often be in conflict with the pastor. Dick, on the other hand, was a steady and calming influence, and to this day is one of my very best friends. As we both moved on to new assignments, Dick and I would often vacation together. When he became a pastor one of his parishioners owned a home in Key West, Florida, and Dick and I would spend a week there every year for about a 15-year period. We both enjoyed our times together in Key West.

I fondly remember telling someone that I could never imagine being anywhere else but at Queen of Peace. The parish was at the forefront of the Vatican II renewal, embracing liturgical changes and introducing deacons to the Archdiocese. The Saint Vincent De Paul Society met weekly, embodying the spirit of service and charity.

Queen of Peace owed its vibrancy and renewal to the people, their priests, and the Daughters of Charity who had come before, leaving a legacy of faith, compassion, and dedication to civil rights and social justice. The time I spent at Queen of Peace was formative and inspiring, influencing my ministry and instilling a deep commitment to serving others with love and devotion. The parish will forever hold a special place in my heart, and I am grateful for the invaluable experiences and lessons it provided and the wonderful people and families who mentored and loved me to enlightenment.

My father passed away in 1972, shortly after he, my mother, and I had visited their homeland and families in both Ireland and England. During the journey, he complained of excessive tiredness, and upon our return to the US in August of that year, he was diagnosed with colon cancer. My father played a significant role in shaping my life and beliefs, leaving a profound impact on me through his journey from humble beginnings in Great Britain to becoming a successful and caring individual in the United States.

His life was a testament to hard work, perseverance, and adaptability. Despite having only a sixth-grade education, he started his life in America by working in wealthy people's homes. From stories and photos, it is evident that he was living his dream and loving his life. After meeting my mother and getting married, my parents began to settle down. He eventually secured a job working for the federal government, specifically in the Lend-Lease Administration, a job he cherished dearly.

However, during the McCarthy hearings in the early 1950s, with the paranoia over communism raging, it came to light that my father had briefly worked as a houseman in the Russian Embassy. As a result, he was forced to resign from his cherished government job. The devastating blow led him to work in various low-level jobs for several years.

Despite these setbacks, my father's determination eventually led him to become a successful salesperson for office furniture supplies. In the last two decades of his life, he managed to pay off our home mortgage and secure some savings. He was a frugal man, and his sensible approach to finances left a lasting impression on me.

Beyond his professional accomplishments, my father had many other talents and qualities. He was well-read and had a gift for playing the piano. In his youth, he led a small band that performed at British American Club activities, as well as British embassy functions. Music was an important part of our home, and my father would play the piano especially when he was feeling a little melancholy. My mother once told me, "Your father likes to play the piano when he's thinking about his mother and sisters in England."

I appreciated my father's common sense and realistic view of the world. While supportive of my pursuits, he would occasionally challenge my beliefs and raise questions about the Catholic Church. Once, when I was halfway through my major seminary education, he cut out an article from the Washington Post that covered the resignation from the priesthood of a well-known and respected Catholic theologian, Father Charles Davis. Davis left the priesthood and renounced the Church for abandoning the vision of the Second Vatican Council. He denounced papal infallibility, the doctrine of the Assumption, and the Church's position on birth control. Having converted to Catholicism as a young man, my father, despite his regular attendance at Mass, identified with Davis' criticism and wanted me to at least hear the other side on certain issues of faith. I think my father was afraid that I was being indoctrinated through my Catholic, and especially my seminary, education.

Looking back, I regret not asking my father about his own life, experiences, and opinions. I wish I had learned more about his journey to America, his youth in England, and how he fell in love with my mother. Nevertheless, the memories of his love for me, his own mother, and our family, and his many kind gestures, like writing letters to his mother and buying me a cherished fountain pen upon my graduation from elementary school remain, etched in my heart.

After my father's passing, my mother remained an unwavering pillar of strength in my life. She chose not to remarry and instead dedicated herself to volunteering at Nativity Church. She taught religion in the Sunday school program, served as a lector and Eucharistic minister during masses, and attended daily noon mass. Despite the challenges life presented her, she remained strong-willed, morally upright, and never hesitated to stand up for what she believed was right.

When she was 70, my mother received a devastating diagnosis of terminal cancer and was given only "a few good months to live." At first, she came to terms with her fate and began dividing up her assets among her three children. However, as time went on and her life showed no signs of imminent death, she resumed living her life as usual, facing each day with courage and resilience. Eventually, in 1996, at the age of 86, she passed away, and the cause of her death was simply attributed to old age.

My mother's charitable nature, community involvement, and love for God were inspirational. She ran a little boarding house which coupled with my father's social security check and her frugal lifestyle, enabled her to live financially independently while finding time to remain engaged in her church and neighborhood activities. As her siblings aged, my mother was there to lend a helping hand, caring for my uncles Michael and Sandy and my aunts Maude, Joan, and Mary in their later years. She also formed strong bonds with her new neighbors as our neighborhood and church demographics changed. An older woman whom I met many years after my mother's death (and she realized I was a priest) told me that one day she was walking up the street in my old neighborhood and my mother was watering the grass. She said my mother said to me, "You look like you would enjoy a cup of tea." She said, "Your mother invited me in for a cup of tea, and she had never met me before;

just saw me in the neighborhood." That was my mother: she was a good neighbor and loved people.

My parents' influence on my life has been immeasurable. My father's journey from a "footman" in Great Britain to a butler in the US, his government service, and his successful career as a salesman, and my mother's unwavering dedication to her family, church, and community, while managing a small business, have shaped my values and perspectives. I am forever grateful for the love and guidance they bestowed upon me.

CHAPTER 6
THE OFFICE OF SOCIAL DEVELOPMENT

"Action on behalf of justice and participation in the transformation of the world fully appear to us as a constitutive dimension of the preaching of the Gospel . . ."

(Populorum Progressio, Paul VI, 1967)

After three fulfilling years as an assistant pastor at Our Lady Queen of Peace, I was asked if I would ever consider working for the Archdiocese. I expressed that my only interest would be in social justice or ecumenism. By coincidence I received a call a few weeks after that from Monsignor Ralph Kuehner, the Director of the Office of Social Development, the office of the Archdiocese that focused on urban affairs, social justice, and ecumenism, offering me the position of Assistant Director.

Accepting the role was another life-changing choice for me. Monsignor Kuehner, a brilliant and caring mentor, allowed me the freedom to grow into the position and even gave me the autonomy to steer the office in ways that I believed were important for the future of the Church. Working in the office introduced me to talented and likeminded individuals who broadened my perspective on ministry and human rights issues.

The Church at that time was still operating in the spirit of the Second Vatican Council, and the possibilities for social justice and community engagement felt endless. Catholics were encouraged to actively engage with the world and work towards building a more just society. This resonated deeply with me, and I became particularly interested in social justice education.

One of my main goals was to help people at the parish level understand the rich social justice teachings and traditions of the Catholic Church. At the Archdiocesan level, I became more outspoken on issues of civil rights, social justice, and peace concerns. The early 1970s was a tumultuous time with the lingering effects of the Vietnam War, civil rights struggles, assassinations of prominent leaders, world hunger, and urban violence. It was a time that demanded action and commitment to social justice causes.

In the office, I collaborated with other dedicated young priests, Catholic nuns, and lay Catholics who shared my passion for social justice. Together, we developed educational tools, conducted workshops, and provided resources for parish small group prayer and action on social justice concerns during Advent and Lent. Our efforts were fueled by a desire to effect positive change and create a more compassionate and just society.

However, during this time, I began to notice a growing backlash among some Catholics, even within the clergy and hierarchy, towards the changes brought about by the Vatican Council, particularly regarding social action. Unfortunately, this was evident in the decrease in funding for our office and projects, which was a source of frustration for Monsignor Kuehner.

As a result, Monsignor Kuehner decided to move on, and a new Director was appointed. Father Sean O'Malley, who is now the Cardinal Archbishop of Boston, took on the role. Although he was a good and committed leader, I felt a yearning to return to pastoral work. I made the difficult decision to resign from my position and asked if I could be assigned as a full-time associate pastor at Saint Augustine Catholic Church.

Thankfully, my request was honored, and I returned to pastoral work with a renewed sense of purpose. The experience in the Office of Social Development had a profound impact on me, shaping my commitment to social justice and my understanding of the Church's role in advocating for a more compassionate and equitable society. I carry the lessons I learned, and the values instilled during that time in my heart as I continue to serve in ministry and strive to make a positive difference in the lives of those I encounter.

One of the highlights of my days in the Office of Social Development was when I met Dorothy Day:

Visiting Dorothy Day at the Catholic Worker Farm in Tivoli, New York, was a transformative experience that left an indelible mark on my heart and soul. I arrived on a Friday, eager to meet this remarkable woman who had devoted her life to serving the poor and marginalized. As soon as I introduced myself to Dorothy, she welcomed me warmly and offered me a room to stay.

Over the course of the next few days, I immersed myself in the loving and caring atmosphere of the Catholic Worker movement. Life at the farm was bustling and somewhat chaotic, yet there was a profound sense of community and purpose. I witnessed firsthand the dedication and compassion with which the members of the Catholic Worker movement served those in need.

Breakfast on Sunday was a poignant moment as it was time to bid farewell to Dorothy. I expressed my gratitude for the hospitality and the opportunity to be part of this incredible community. With a smile, she asked me about my work in Washington, DC. Somewhat proudly, I replied, "I'm the Assistant Director of the Office of Social Development of the Archdiocese of Washington." I expected her to be impressed by my position, but her response was a gentle yet powerful reminder of her unwavering principles.

"Oh no," she said, "I want to know what you are doing for the poor and the homeless." In that moment, Dorothy Day's authenticity and dedication shone through. She was not interested in titles or prestige; all that mattered to her was the impact one had on the lives of those in need. Her question struck a chord in my heart, and I realized the importance of aligning my actions with my beliefs.

Dorothy's lesson had a profound effect on me, and I never forgot it. Her commitment to the poor and marginalized was genuine and unwavering, serving as a constant reminder of what truly matters in life. When I returned to Washington, DC, I wrote her a heartfelt thank you note, expressing my gratitude for the wisdom she imparted.

To my surprise, I received a response from Dorothy in the form of a Catholic Worker postcard and an encouraging note. Her words affirmed my dedication to social justice and renewed my commitment to serving the less fortunate. I cherished her note, knowing that one day, when Dorothy Day is canonized as a Saint in the Catholic Church, it would be a precious relic for me.

Visiting Dorothy Day and experiencing the Catholic Worker movement firsthand was a pivotal moment in my life. It reinforced my understanding of the true essence of service and compassion and deepened my resolve to dedicate myself to the needs of the poor and marginalized. Dorothy Day's legacy continues to inspire me, and her lessons remain etched in my heart as I strive to make a positive impact on the lives of others, just as she did throughout her extraordinary life.

During my tenure in the Office of Social Development, I had the privilege of participating in a national conference focused on social justice and urban ministry. This annual event, hosted by the University of Notre Dame, was sponsored by the Catholic Committee on Urban Ministry (CCUM) and established by Monsignor Jack Egan, a highly esteemed Chicago priest dedicated to advocating for social justice and civil rights. Through CCUM I became acquainted with a national network of Catholic clergy, religious men and women, and lay Catholics committed to effecting social change.

In addition to attending these conferences personally, I facilitated access to them for our office staff and parish workers within the Archdiocese of Washington. Reflecting on these experiences and my work with CCUM, I've come to realize that I gained more than I contributed. Looking back, I understand that each of these experiences served as a stepping stone, providing me with valuable insights and increased wisdom that I could apply to my pastoral work, teaching, and preaching.

CHAPTER 7
ST. AUGUSTINE, THE GOSPEL CHOIR, IMPAC

"Lead me, guide me along the way,

For if you lead me, I cannot stray.

Lord, let me walk each day with Thee.

Lead me, O Lord, lead me."

(Doris Akers, gospel singer)

When I went to work for the Office of Social Development I moved from the rectory of Our Lady Queen of Peace to an "in residence" position at the Shrine of the Sacred Heart in Northwest Washington DC. The balance between residence and full-time duties at the Office proved to be a challenge. Because I was replacing an associate pastor at Sacred Heart there was an expectation that I would be assuming a significant portion of his ministerial duties. Navigating the demands of my new position in the Archdiocese and the expectations at Sacred Heart was difficult.

Although the time spent at Sacred Heart was enjoyable, living with good and committed priests, and once again meeting and working with faith-filled parishioners, I often felt that I was letting people down and not carrying my weight in the parish. The Shrine of the Sacred Heart, once renowned as one of the largest and wealthiest parishes in the Archdiocese, had witnessed its congregation undergo transformations due to shifting demographics within the city. The aftermath of Dr. King's assassination and the subsequent civil upheavals prompted the departure of numerous older parishioners, ushering in a more diverse assembly, including a growing Latino population. I contributed by offering daily and Sunday Masses for the English-speaking population as my schedule permitted.

After residing at Sacred Heart for a few years I made a transition to Saints Paul and Augustine Parish in 1976, just a few blocks down the street, where I became a resident while continuing to work for the Archdiocese. My friendship with Father Ray Kemp, coupled with our shared vision for parish ministry, was instrumental in this move. Father Kemp, who had recently been appointed pastor of Sts. Paul and Augustine welcomed me into the role as a resident. As before I assisted with daily and Sunday Masses.

The initial years at Sts. Paul and Augustine proved to be enlightening and enriching. Father Kemp, a beloved figure within the parish and the neighborhood, had been a steadfast presence since his ordination in 1967. He exhibited an insightful grasp of African-American culture and history, serving as both an inspiration and a mentor. Through his guidance, I learned more about the intricacies of the African-American community, particularly the African-American Catholic Community.

The parish however grappled with an aging congregation as integration led many African American Catholics to move to other churches and neighborhoods. These shifts were echoed in the city's evolving demographics, with the surrounding area of Sts. Paul and Augustine experiencing economic decline. The epicenter of the civil disturbances after the assassination of Dr. King was 14th and U Streets, NW, placing the church and school within the heart of what was considered one of Washington's most distressed neighborhoods.

During this period the congregation predominantly consisted of elderly individuals, many of whom were stalwart Catholics who had confronted the challenges of segregation within society and the Church. Among them was Pauline Jones, a remarkable woman whose influence on me was profound. Pauline exhibited a specific interest in assessing my suitability for ministry within the African American community. Our shared visits to homebound elderly parishioners deepened our connection, as she extended her respect and friendship.

During our time together Pauline recounted her personal experiences growing up in the Church and in America. As a lifelong and devout Catholic, she had received the sacraments of baptism, first holy communion, confirmation, and marriage at the historic Saint Augustine Church – a cornerstone of Black Catholicism. My friendship with Pauline grew, nurtured by her candid revelations regarding her feelings about the fates of numerous "White priests" she deemed to be in hell due to their racial prejudices. When I asked her once why she was always telling me about the White priests in hell, she said, "Because I don't want you to be one of them." I love Pauline Jones because of her honesty and her trust in me.

I should mention here that the neighborhood once housed two distinct Catholic churches: one for White Catholics, St. Paul, and another for African-American Catholics, St. Augustine. After the demographic shifts initiated by the Brown v. Board of Education ruling in 1954, both parishes saw diminishing congregations. In response, the Archdiocese consolidated the two parishes, forming Sts. Paul and Augustine Parish, which centered its worship in the old Saint Paul Church at 15th and Vee Streets, NW, while keeping the school and convent at the St. Augustine location at 15th and Tee Streets, NW.

In 1976 when I arrived at Sts. Paul and Augustine, we were operating two parish locations. Father Kemp, with the encouragement of the parish council, astutely sold off the old St. Augustine property and channeled the profits toward renovating the St. Paul school and church, as well as procuring a townhouse for the new convent. This strategic move was pivotal, aligning Fr. Kemp's vision for an invigorated urban parish.

To recruit younger parishioners and breathe new life into the congregation, Fr. Kemp hired a recent Howard University graduate, Leon Roberts, to establish a Gospel Choir, which at the time was unheard of in Catholic churches. Once after the Gospel Choir was bringing more and more young people to the church, a young man who had grown up in the parish but had moved away came back and was blown away by what he experienced. He asked me, "Does the Pope know what is going on in this church?"

Leon Roberts, the Gospel Choir, the consolidation of the properties, and the renovations all were taking place as I arrived in 1976. Our communal endeavors were rooted in a beautiful Gothic church, a renovated school, a revitalized Gingras Community Center, a rectory accommodating three priests, and a convent for the Oblate Sisters of Providence – dedicated educators of African American children – staffing the school. Father Kemp's vision was materializing as a vibrant urban parish, embracing change and renewal. Sts. Paul and Augustine was truly a Vatican II parish.

Upon resigning from my position as Assistant Director of the Office of Social Development in 1978, I assumed a new role as associate pastor at Sts. Paul and Augustine. In doing so I became fully immersed in the life of the parish, embracing its rich history. As our congregation grew, drawn to our vibrant style of worship led by our Gospel Choir and our acceptance of a younger gay community, I saw the potential to realize my own vision of a dynamic church built on the principles of Vatican II.

Again, due much to the interests of Father Kemp the parish was closely connected to Mackin Catholic High School, an Archdiocesan secondary school serving a predominantly African American student population. During this period, a young teacher at Mackin developed a retreat program which he called IMPAC, centered on improving the students' and teachers' personal relationships with the Risen Christ. It was an intense weekend experience focusing on the themes of Christ's paschal experience while using symbols and music relevant to Black culture. I participated in a couple of these IMPAC retreats and recognized their potential for fostering a strong sense of community among our adult parishioners. I encouraged Father Kemp to integrate the IMPAC model into a parish retreat program, which he did and it became highly successful.

Over the next 15 or so years, approximately 500 parishioners, including members of the gospel and traditional choirs, engaged in the IMPAC retreat experience. This movement played a pivotal role in the ongoing revitalization of Sts. Paul and Augustine Church.

In 1981, Cardinal James Hickey, the Archbishop of Washington, recognized the creative talents of Fr. Kemp and promoted him to the role of Secretary of Pastoral Life for the archdiocese. This elevation left the position of pastor vacant. Fr. Kemp recommended me to succeed him and after an interview with the Cardinal and one of our auxiliary bishops, I was appointed the pastor of Sts. Paul and Augustine Church. I like to tell the story that at the interview prior to my appointment the auxiliary bishop asked me what it was like to preach on Sunday at a parish knowing there were so many gay people in the congregation. I answered, "I've always wondered what it was like preaching at Little Flower Church knowing there were so many rich people in the congregation." The Cardinal said, "John, it's not the same."

At the time of my appointment, I became the youngest pastor in the Archdiocese. I was 38 years old. This wasn't attributed to any exceptional personal prowess but rather arose from the scarcity of priests with training for, or interest in, ministering in the African-American community.

Shortly after my appointment, one of the associate pastors departed to pursue further studies. In response, I asked another young priest, Mike Kelley, to join me in the endeavor. In addition, I brought on a business manager and a stipend volunteer tasked with outreach work.

A longstanding friend from my elementary school days, who had since become a successful businessperson in the city, generously offered to cover the salary of a community organizer for the parish. With a dedicated team comprising the director of music, the school principal, the Sunday school principal, the parish administrator, the outreach worker, the community organizer, Father Mike Kelley as the associate pastor, and myself as the pastor, we embarked on a collaborative journey. We conducted weekly meetings and worked closely alongside the parish council to establish a shared vision. This concerted effort allowed us to consistently advance the development of a vibrant center city parish.

When it was announced that I was becoming pastor, my childhood mentor, Monsignor Jim Montgomery, who was pastor of one of Washington's more prestigious and well-off parishes, called me and offered to fund a professional fundraising organization to run an increased offertory campaign for the parish. This was a godsend in that our parishioners responded with great enthusiasm and our revenue began to increase dramatically.

Since the civil disturbances pretty much destroyed the business district along 14th Street the neighborhood continued to experience a significant decline, transforming into one of the city's most plagued neighborhoods. It became notorious for prostitution, the sale and use of illegal drugs (including crack cocaine), and the beginning of gun violence. Despite the grim state of the neighborhood, the church was undergoing a remarkable resurgence. The adjacent school was also serving as a safe haven for our families and children.

From my perspective, the church and school were beacons of hope in some very depressing and dark times in our city. Sunday services began to attract an ever-growing congregation, to the extent that parking scarcity emerged as a notable problem. We began hiring security for evening and night events, to help with the parking problem and give people some sense of security walking back and forth from their cars. Mayor Marion Barry in an effort to change the image of the neighborhood decided to build a multi-story municipal center on the corner of 14th and U Streets, presenting the parish with an opportunity to advocate for the construction of affordable housing for larger families.

An innovative idea took shape as we identified four abandoned and dilapidated townhouses on V Street, situated across from the school. I engaged the mayor inquiring about the possibility of redeveloping these buildings to accommodate larger families. To Mayor Barry's credit, he embraced the concept, leading to the redesign of the municipal building to include the space where the four townhouses stood. This shift in design paved the way for us to collaborate with a developer who, working with the city, constructed an apartment building, named the Gino Baroni Apartments, to cater to low- and moderate-income families.

Gino Baroni at one time had been an associate pastor at Sts. Paul and Augustine before rising to the position of Assistant Secretary in the Department of Housing and Urban Development. Interestingly the developer of the project was the same individual who had supported our community organizer.

Our community involvement extended beyond housing initiatives. While Fr. Kemp was still pastor, he had begun organizing the community to address concerns like housing, crime, education, and displacement from the beginning of gentrification. Our volunteer outreach worker continued the process and with other community leaders formed the 14th and U Street Coalition which met regularly in our Gingras Center. As a show of solidarity, the 14th & U Coalition held an annual Reclaim Our Neighborhood Festival to bring our community together and support local small businesses.

With the leadership of our parish council, we also began to tackle broader issues such as racial inequality, racism, and even Apartheid in South Africa. We became actively involved in the Free South Africa movement. During Fr. Kemp's pastorship the parish council agreed to place a sign on the front lawn of the church with the words "Free South Africa," which also served to distinguish our parish and attract people who were engaged in social justice and human rights issues. One of our dedicated parish council members played a pivotal role in establishing "Black Coffee," an educational advocacy program fostering dialogue and workshops on matters of civil rights and African-American history. We engaged speakers from Howard University and even fostered a sister church relationship with a large Afrocentric Catholic church in Soweto, South Africa. A particularly impactful event occurred when our auditorium was filled to capacity and we established a telephone connection with leaders from the South African Regina Mundi Catholic Church. We also welcomed Archbishop Hurley a South African bishop who was an outspoken critic of Apartheid.

The Free South Africa movement involved daily antiapartheid protests outside the South African Embassy. Activists, including ministers, priests, and other religious leaders engaged in civil disobedience to advocate the end of apartheid and the liberation of South Africa. As part of these protests, I and two others on our staff were arrested. We were quickly freed and no charges were brought, but my arrest did come back to bite me when later as a fundraiser for Carroll High School I discovered I was barred from certain federal buildings including the White House and the Treasury Department.

During these years we also welcomed other notable speakers, including Rev. Jesse Jackson, Congressman Walter Fauntroy, Sister Thea Bowman, Archbishop Denis Hurley, and many distinguished professors, clergy, and bishops who addressed issues related to African-American and pan-African concerns.

Shortly after I became pastor one of our young leaders, John Butler, pulled me aside before Mass one Sunday and smiling pointed to the packed congregation and said, "Mudd, look out there at all that talent; get out of the way!" What John was saying and what I sensed in my gut was that my role as a White priest in a Black congregation was to enable the tremendous talent among our parishioners, let them take ownership, and facilitate their abilities for the greater good. I had always resented a top-down model of leadership, often voiced in the Catholic Church with the words, "because I'm the bishop or because I'm the pastor." I believed then, and I believe even more strongly now, that authority and power come from the bottom up, and the strength of any church comes from the people and not the leadership. The role of leadership is to get out of the way and let the Spirit guide the people in the work of building God's Kingdom. I believe that St. Augustine Church became such a dynamic community because our clergy and leadership team understood that the parish was the people and when the people believed they had ownership they responded with enthusiasm and generosity. Pope Francis calls this model "synodality," and it is based on consultation, dialogue, and action in the spirit of the Gospel.

Of course, there are boundaries: The Catholic Church is a hierarchical church and we understand that the hierarchy has responsibility for teaching and protecting the deposit of faith. Pastors stand as a safeguard to keep congregations from doing anything that would contradict Catholic dogma or the teaching authority of our Pope and bishops. I often said if it doesn't contradict official Church teaching, and we have the funds, why not!? One of our parishioners once challenged me over a handicapped entrance to the church. He said the parish council agreed on it and you haven't done it. I said, as soon as the parish council approves the budget and as soon as we have the money it will get done. I always insisted that the council and leadership team agree on an annual budget and live by it accordingly.

Once, when our gospel choir agreed to sing at a concert at the Metropolitan Community Church of Washington, DC (MCCDC), a Protestant denomination of LGBTQ people, I intervened to cancel our participation. Although I didn't have any personal problem with our participation, I knew the presence of our St. Augustine Catholic Church choir could easily have been misinterpreted as an endorsement of the mission of MCCDC. I was criticized widely, by some of my own congregation, by the Washington Post, the Washington Blade (the oldest LGBTQ newspaper in the US), the TV media, and even by an editorial in the Catholic Standard (the Archdiocese of Washington's newspaper). I should add that the editor of the Standard was let go shortly after that incident. I argued that our parish could be outspoken on every civil and human rights issue, but we had to be cautious on any issues related to the Catholic Church's position on sexual ethics.

As the gospel choir grew in numbers and more instruments were being added to accompany them, it was obvious we needed to expand our sanctuary. Again, with the guidance of the parish council, we decided to make some major renovations to the church. We did a yearlong study and agreed to enlarge the sanctuary making room for a 50-member choir, and musical instruments, including a grand piano, and a new electronic organ. We moved the Blessed Sacrament to a side altar, brought the main altar out further into the congregation, and turned some of the front pews toward the center to create more of a sense of community gathered around the altar and the pulpit. We had a beautiful marble pulpit from the historic St. Augustine Church set in a place of prominence next to the altar thus creating a balance between the symbols for the Sacrament and the Word. There were old "Jim Crow" pews in the back of the St. Paul church which we brought to the front as pews of honor for our elderly parishioners. We also installed a newly stained glass widow commemorating a conversation Sts. Monica and Augustine had before Augustine's departure for Africa. Monica and Augustine were depicted as Africans. Finally, we installed an immersion baptismal pool which conformed to the Vatican Council's directive for the renewal of adult baptism. As part of the immersion pool and as a water feed to the pool we inset the baptismal font that also came from the old historic St. Augustine Church.

During the renovation process, a humorous incident unfolded. While I was standing in the old marble pulpit and trying to decide exactly where and how it should be positioned, Josephine Chase, an elderly parishioner who, like Pauline Jones, had endured the challenges of racism in society and Church, strolled down the aisle, looked up at me with a steady gaze, and said, "Father Mudd, when you get up there on Sunday, you better have something to say." Every time after that, whenever I stood in that hallowed pulpit, I asked the Lord to give me something to say that would touch the hearts of our good parishioners.

Because of the history of segregation in Washington, and because St. Paul was at one time a White Catholic church that had embraced the separation of the races and even had Jim Crow seating, at my recommendation the parish council petitioned the Cardinal to have the name of the church changed from Sts. Paul and Augustine to Saint Augustine. He agreed and the old St. Paul parish was suppressed and the parish of St. Augustine was reestablished as the Mother Church of Black Catholics in the District of Columbia. All of these changes were made by consensus and with the approval of the parish council.

Two other programs played a significant role in the parish's liturgical renewal and sacramental practices: The RCIA (Rite of Christian Initiation for Adults) and the Returning Catholics program. Again, Father Kemp had been a driving force behind the initiation of the RCIA. He saw it as an opportunity to bring adult converts into the Church through a year-long process of initiation that included instruction, dialogue, prayer, and reflection, all in a communal setting. The Returning Catholics Program grew out of the RCIA in that more and more lapsed Catholics wanted to go through a similar process. The two programs, although similar in process, were distinct in the people that they included. I understood the importance of both these processes and engaged fully in support once I became the pastor.

Fr. Mike Kelley was a godsend to the parish in that he too had a progressive vision of what a dynamic urban parish could be. He worked diligently in every effort, including the Sunday School, Marriage Encounter, IMPAC, the RCIA, the Retreat and Confirmation program for teenagers, the Family Camp, and the sacramental life of the parish. I understood why Jesus sent his disciples out "two by two," because I can't imagine being pastor of St. Augustine without Fr. Mike Kelley at my side every step of the way.

Others who were on the staff during my time as pastor, and who were invaluable in our success, were: Linda Wallace (Business Manager), Dominic Moulden (Community Organizer), Diane Williams (Community Outreach / 14th and U Sts. Coalition), John Butler (RCIA, Returning Catholics, IMPAC), and Betty Washington (Sunday School). Mike Riley, Steve Benefield, Louis Grillo, and Manual Gaffney were other young parishioners upon whom I relied heavily for support. Towards the end of my administration, we welcomed another dynamic young priest, Fr. John Payne OSA. John was a gifted preacher and immediately became an integral part of the leadership team and the parish. Unfortunately, John died at a very young age, soon after being appointed Principal of the Duke Ellington School of the Performing Arts. After I left St. Augustine John moved away from full-time pastoral work and became a faculty member, vice principal, and principal before his untimely death.

I would be remiss if I did not mention St. Augustine School and the Oblate Sisters of Providence. The Oblates were founded by Mother Mary Elizabeth Lange in 1829 in Baltimore, for the education of girls of African descent. It was the first permanent community of Black Catholic sisters in the United States. They were themselves African American and they desired to teach Black children who had been excluded from educational opportunities during slavery and in the aftermath. By the 1950s there were 500 Oblate sisters administering schools throughout the South and in the Dominican Republic and Costa Rica. The Oblates staffed St. Augustine almost from its inception and I had the privilege of collaborating with the sisters during my time in the parish. I admired the valuable work carried out by these remarkable women, and in my time as pastor, I had the opportunity to work alongside two exceptional principals, Sister Barbara Spears, and Sister Ricardo Maddox. These two natural leaders displayed a genuine affection for the children and their families. They effectively managed the school, overseeing the hiring of teachers, tuition collection, teaching the students, and embodying examples of strong Black women of faith for our parish and neighborhood. As our community continued to grow, and while I was actively engaged with the pastoral work of running a large parish and at the same time engaging in neighborhood activities, the Oblate Sisters took charge of our school, maintaining the tradition and mission of educating Black children.

The success that we achieved at St. Augustine would not have been possible without the unwavering support of our parishioners, guided by an elected parish council. We were fortunate to be blessed with numerous dedicated lay leaders, both young and old, who willingly shouldered the mantle of leadership. Upon their election to council positions, they wholeheartedly embraced the parish's mission. Every year the staff would go on a two-day retreat to plan for the following year, and the parish council also had an annual planning retreat. The staff and council worked hand in hand to implement a common vision

I held steadfast to the belief that the Finance Committee of the Council should spearhead the efforts in creating and overseeing the yearly budget. Throughout my tenure, this committee performed admirably and with a high level of professionalism.

Also, during my tenure as pastor, we initiated a Capital Campaign. Our very generous parishioners pledged over $2 million in response. That Campaign eventually funded the replacement of the church's HVAC system and for the first time, St. Augustine Church was air-conditioned.

On a very sad note, my time as pastor was also marked by the revelation that HIV AIDS was attacking gay men, and because our congregation had a large percentage of LGBTQ parishioners, we were particularly hard hit. The disease was devastating the Washington DC gay community, and we lost too many young gifted men to death. Thank God that we have a handle on the disease as a society, but back then we were just discovering the immensity of the problem as our congregation suffered through death after death.

In the entire history of St. Augustine Church, there was never a Black pastor. Younger Black priests were coming up through the ranks of the Archdiocese and I believed that my replacement should be a Black pastor. Finally, in 1990 I asked to be reassigned and the first Black pastor of St. Augustine Church was appointed. There was a headline in the religion section of the Washington Post that read, "Finally A Black Pastor!"

My years at St. Augustine could not have been happier. I loved everything about the parish, the people I worked with, the neighborhood, the exciting style of worship, and our engagement in social justice and civil rights, but most of all I loved the people of our parish who I admired for their strong faith and their endurance in the face of such adversity experienced in a racist society and church. After 14 years, however, I knew it was time to move on.

When I left St. Augustine, there was a farewell Mass and reception and I received many accolades but perhaps none touched me more than the one I received from one of our very active young parishioners, who had gone through the RCIA program and became Catholic during my tenure. He was the one who initiated the "Black Coffee" program and served on the parish council. I include his note here because it sums up what I hoped to be as a pastor of my beloved St. Augustine Parish:

Dear Father John Mudd,

We now say fond farewell to you as pastor of our dear St. Augustine Church. On behalf of the present and past members of the Committee on Africa and the Diaspora, I say thank you for the continued, consistent support and encouragement that you have given us over the ten years of our commitment and work.

We praise God for giving this Church and this committee a shepherd-servant like you. Through much haze you have persisted in seeing the light o'er yonder far hills – the light of social, racial, and economic justice, and PEACE.

May the Lord continue to be with you and guide you throughout your life.

Sincerely,

Ernest CHKA Withers, Jr.

October 20, 1990

CHAPTER 8

ARCHBISHOP CARROLL HIGH SCHOOL / FORT BELVOIR

"We don't teach them because they are Catholic; we teach them because we are Catholic."

(Cardinal James Hickey)

In 1978, during my residence at Sts. Paul and Augustine, Pope John Paul I passed away unexpectedly after a short papacy of around 70 days. He was succeeded by Polish Cardinal Karol Wojtyla, who adopted the name Pope John Paul II. His papal tenure continued until his death in April 2005. Soon after Pope John Paul II assumed office, the Vatican's Congregation for the Doctrine of the Faith notified Hans Kung, a renowned Catholic theologian and one of the theological advisors at the Second Vatican Council, that he was no longer recognized as a Catholic theologian. This decision was prompted by certain theological viewpoints of his that were found to be incongruent with official Catholic doctrine. At that time, I believed it was just a matter of time before the Vatican's conservative perspectives would influence local parishes.

I identified with Hans Kung and other forward-thinking figures within the Church, and much of my work as pastor at St. Augustine aligned with these progressive ideas. It didn't take long for my expectations to materialize, as the Church's direction turned more conservative and regressive.

Archbishop Joseph Ratzinger, who held the leadership of the Congregation for the Doctrine of the Faith under John Paul II, had shifted from his prior progressive stance as a theological advisor at Vatican II to become notably more reactionary and conservative. Over the course of several years, the vision of Vatican II was increasingly curtailed, and a rising number of conservative bishops were appointed across the globe. Seminaries began producing priests in the mold of John Paul II, following a pre-Vatican II paradigm. Consequently, many of the pastoral reforms that had been implemented were pushed into the background.

While we had indeed established something unique at St. Augustine, it became apparent to me that we were starting to be regarded with doubt. I believe that my successor as the pastor was instructed to restore order to the parish. Given this atmosphere, I sensed that introducing my vision of the Church to a different parish would pose significant challenges. Coincidently, around this time, an opportunity emerged for a Director of Development role (focused on fundraising) at my high school alma mater.

At the same time, however, numerous Catholic schools catering to Black students were shutting down. There were various factors contributing to this trend, yet in my perspective, the primary reason was the Church's failure to make essential adaptations to financially support and maintain such institutions. In 1989, seven Catholic secondary schools in the Archdiocese of Washington were shuttered, with five of the seven being consolidated into the one remaining school in the city limits, Archbishop Carroll High School. Because I had some success in fundraising at St. Augustine, I believed I could be instrumental in raising funds for Carroll ensuring its long-term success. I thought that if alumni and the broader Catholic community were challenged, they would respond with generous support.

I volunteered to go to the high school and take over its fledging fund-raising office. What I didn't expect was the resistance I would face. Once the merger of the high schools took place Carroll transitioned from an all-boys integrated to a coed and virtually all the Black student population. The White male alumni reacted by saying it wasn't their school any longer. And interestingly many Black alumni reacted the same; "not the school I attended." I was also replacing a Vice President who had been a legendary coach, Counsellor, and administrator at the school. My job was challenging and I met a lot of resistance at first, but soon through persistence and with the encouragement of some of our older alums and the help of a small dedicated staff the Office of Advancement became more and more successful, and over my twenty-four years as Director of the Office we raised $32 million.

John Badaczewski, a teacher and coach, had transitioned into an assistant in the fund-raising office and was a big help in welcoming me and introducing me to alumni. To his credit the office had maintained a database of alumni, albeit on index cards, but nevertheless a pretty accurate list with current addresses and phone numbers. At that time there was no such thing as the Internet or email, so pretty much all contacts were made by mail or phone. I managed to get a grant of $10,000 from the Bureau of Black and Indian Missions and we purchased four computers and moved our database from the index cards to a computerized system. Interestingly, shortly after I purchased the computers the president of Carroll, Fr. George Murry, SJ, got a call from the Secretary of Education in the Archdiocese reprimanding him for spending $10,000 on computers without the permission of the bishop's representative. Fr. Murry in turn told me that from then on I should get his permission before spending any large sums of money. I told Fr. Murry, "You hired the wrong guy; I'm not asking permission to do what I think is necessary for the good of my small operation, especially after I solicited the funding and for the specific purpose of purchasing computers." After that Fr. Murry and his successors at Carroll pretty much left me alone to run the fundraising office as I saw fit.

John Badaczewski introduced me to two young alumni, Dave and Mark Savercool, who actually coached our small staff on the purchase and use of the computers. Within a few years, I hired Mark to be my assistant. He worked with me at Carroll for 8 years before moving to another Catholic high school, Gonzaga, to be their Director of Development. When I retired in 2013 Mark came back to Carroll as my replacement and is doing an outstanding job. In fact, at his initiative, Carroll is undertaking a capital campaign with a $25 million goal.

Also, around the time I arrived at Carroll in 1990, Father Murry hired an Administrative Assistant for his office of President and my Office of Director of Development, Dana Peters. I remember telling Dana that she and her husband, Joe, and I were going to grow old together. We did!!! Joe Dana and I became good friends. Joe died in 2017 And Dana died in 2021. I turned 80 in 2023.

Sister Helen McCulloch came to Carroll in the Guidance Office around the same time in 1990 and she and Dana also became good friends. Dana, Joe, and I even visited Helen in her family home in Florida once. Helen retired in 2021.

The Augustinian Friars had administered and taught at Carroll since its opening in 1951 and lived in a residence wing of the school. When the schools merged in 1989 part of the residence wing was converted into space for a couple of classrooms and guidance counselors, as well as administrative offices including development, finance, and the president's office. The upper floor of the old residence wing was rented out to students studying at Catholic University. I lived on that floor during my first year at Carroll. The second year Father Bill Montgomery, another diocesan priest and Faculty member and I cordoned off a section of that floor and created two apartments with a shared kitchen and sitting area. We lived there for 20 years. Bill and I had many laughs together as he and I shared our experiences at the school and in the Archdiocese. Bill was another good priest who I had the fortune to know and live with. He was generous beyond measure. One night when I locked myself out of my apartment, Bill and I got an extension ladder and together manipulated the ladder through the building, out onto the roof of the chapel, and up to my room on the third floor. We argued about who would climb the ladder. I said, "Bill, if the police come and see a Black man climbing up, they will shoot you; they won't shoot me." I climbed the ladder and got into my apartment. It was 12:30 AM on a Sunday morning. I always said it was "dumb and dumber" manipulating that ladder.

I worked with many good people at Carroll. John Badaczewski, Dana Peters, Mark Savercool, Muktar Kelati, Luke Hester, Crystal Rucker, Stacy Rubens, and Jeff Penn, and many more. Luke Hester was a volunteer who came to Carroll after he retired from the Federal Government. His career was in journalism and he was invaluable in the advice he offered and his willingness to help in any effort, including preparing the script for our emcees at our annual Spring Benefit at the Kennedy Center. Muktar Kelat was a young man who came to Carroll to work for a special program that our president at the time, John Butler, designed to reach out to the Washington business community. When that program lost funding, I hired Muktar to work in the development office. Once I asked him to send a Christmas greeting to our 10,000-member database and he sent out the greeting, "Marry Christmas, etc." I said, "Muktar, how could you mistake Marry for Merry?" He said, "Father Mudd, I'm a Muslim and English is my second language. What do you expect?" We laughed and we still laugh over that little typo! Luke, once said when leaving a staff meeting, "Keep the faith!" Muktar replied, "Which one?" Muktar helped me to appreciate Islam as one of the great world religions. He told me many stories of how his father formed him in his faith and taught him to appreciate other people's religions as well.

Luke and Muktar have also become good lifelong friends. Luke coined the phrase: "Muktar, Mark, Luke, and John," a play on the four Gospel writers, and commenting on the four of us working together to advance the mission of Carroll. I can't say enough about Mark Savercool. From almost day one, when John Badaczewski introduced Mark and his brother, Dave, to me, Mark has been a right hand, and a good friend. He made me look good as the director of the office, and now he has taken his rightful place in charge and is doing better than I could have ever dreamed of doing.

I recruited Crystal Rucker and Stacy Rubens, both Carroll grads, to work for the office, Crystal as the director of alumni affairs and Stacy as the director of data and donor management. Again, both were great additions to our team and both have gone on to work in development for other organizations, at better pay, I might add. One of the challenges of Catholic education is being able to offer fair wages to get and keep quality talent.

I can tell many funny stories about fundraising, like the time I was going to ask a famous alum for a generous donation. I stopped along the way to give some money to a homeless man. I asked the man if he believed in God. He said he did and I asked him to pray for me because I was going to ask someone for money. The homeless man said, "You ought to take me, I ask for money all the time." Weeks later I was driving down the street and saw the same homeless man, so I pulled over, gave him some money, and asked if he remembered me. He said, "Are you the guy who asked me to pray for him; you were going to ask someone for money, right?" I told him I was that guy. He said, "How did you do?" I said, "I got $30,000." He said, "Holy shit!! $30,000!!!!"

On another occasion, I asked a successful alum for a donation and he said, "I wouldn't give a penny to that school." I asked why, and he said, "I could barely read when I got out of there." I said, "I could barely read either, but I didn't blame the school. I thought it was my parents' gene pool." He ended up funding a full scholarship for one of our students.

All in all, I found people to be very generous. One of our most generous donors had no affiliation with the school, other than he wanted to help underserved kids. He was an avid horse-racing fan and ended up naming horses after one of the presidents of Carroll and another horse after me. So, two horses, "President Butler," and "Father Mudd," ran at local tracks and the winning proceeds were donated to Carroll. That same friend gave $5 million to fund a Media Center named after a local news anchor, Jim Vance. Unfortunately, both he and his wife died recently, she in 2022 and he in 2023.

When I retired another very generous donor and alum started an endowed scholarship in my name with an initial gift of $1 million. I could go on and on and talk about all the good people and alumni who donated to Carroll over my years as director and now under Mark Savercool's leadership. In the fundraising world, we are told about 80% of your donations come from 20% of your constituents, and I can testify to the truth of that. One of the challenges at Carroll was always to help our alumni understand that even though the demographic of the school has changed over the years, the mission remains the same, and as with every other private institution and school, the success of Carroll depends on our constituents having a sense of ownership and responding appropriately.

As with all my parish assignments during my priesthood, I enjoyed my colleagues, the alumni, and the many friends I worked with during my Carroll years. I believed in the mission of the school, first as an integrated Catholic school and then as a predominantly and primarily Black school. Carroll had a unique place in the Catholic educational landscape and I was very happy to be a part of the school for 24 years. When I graduated from Carroll in 1961, I would have never imagined coming back, but as it is said, "We plan and God laughs." Carroll has been such an important part of my life, and I do bleed Green and Gold!

When I left St. Augustine and came to Carroll in 1990, I moved into the residential wing of the school, the dormitory for the Augustinian priests who taught there before and during my time as a student. As there were fewer and fewer Augustinian priests the rooms were rented out over the years to graduate student-priests at Catholic university. One Sunday morning a priest living in the residence, a Catholic Army chaplain working for the Military Archdiocese, asked me if I had a weekend pastoral assignment. When I said I didn't, he encouraged me to call the chaplain at Fort Belvoir and offer my services. Following his advice, I reached out to the Fort Belvoir chaplain who promptly invited me to cover a couple of Masses the following weekend.

I had reservations, given my history as an advocate for justice and peace and my anti-Vietnam War stance in the 1960s. Furthermore, I questioned my adaptability to a predominantly White community, having been so deeply engaged in ministry in the Black church for a substantial period. Nevertheless, I accepted the challenge and journeyed out to Fort Belvoir.

Contrary to my expectations and stereotypes, I was immediately embraced by a diverse military community and

I found myself enjoying the ministry immensely. The Catholic community at Fort Belvoir soon became my church family. Initially, I made a conscious decision not to become too involved for fear that it would take away from my primary mission doing fundraising for the school. I even decided not to try to learn names, but rather to just focus on giving impactful sermons and leading prayerful liturgical celebrations. However, as time passed, my connection with the community deepened and I found myself more and more invested.

During my last couple of years at St. Augustine, we had a visiting African priest who when celebrating Sunday Mass would recite the gospel reading from memory. I could see how attentive the congregation was to his delivery so I decided to do the same at Fort Belvoir. For the next two decades, I recited the gospel reading at every Sunday Mass from memory. It was a wonderful way to connect with the parishioners, get the attention of the young, and remind people that the Word of Scripture was rooted in the oral traditions of storytelling. With the changes in translations, making memorization more challenging, and the emphasis of the hierarchy on more structured liturgical celebrations, I eventually transitioned back to reading the Gospel from the printed text.

At the high school, one of our teachers led a very successful chocolate drive, the proceeds of which he used for specific student projects. On one of my very first Sundays at Fort Belvoir, I offered my allotment of chocolate bars for sale after mass. This small gesture had an unexpected chain of events. The chaplain informed me that fundraisers were prohibited on military premises but with the consent of the parish council he proposed an alternative to assist my work, and an annual designated offering was initiated, generating significant support for the scholarship fund at Archbishop Carroll High School. From the $72 I made on the sale of the first two boxes of chocolate in 1990 the Fort Belvoir Catholic Community has consistently donated approximately $10,000 per year for the last 30 or more years.

The Catholic Community also supported my efforts at Carroll in a considerable number of other ways, including individual donations and attendance at the school's annual Spring Benefit at the Kennedy Center. I can't say enough about the wonderful people I met at Fort Belvoir, their strong faith, their patriotism, and their desire to serve their country and to give good Catholic witness in their lives. I have made lasting friends at Fort Belvoir and enjoy every time I am with this loving community. The military community is conservative by nature, but they have always listened and been receptive, although not necessarily in agreement, to my more liberal views. In addition, I have found the Catholic community at Belvoir to be always respectful, of my emphasis on the Church's social doctrine and a more socially oriented interpretation of scripture.

During my time at Fort Belvoir, a few significant events took place which changed the nature of the community. Of greatest note was the 9/11 terrorist attacks on the Twin Towers in New York and the Pentagon. Prior to these tragedies, the security measures were relatively lax, making access to the base quite straightforward. After the attacks there was a substantial increase in security protocols, leading to heightened restrictions on entry for individuals without military identification. This shift in security procedures resulted in a noticeable decline in attendance and active participation in Catholic events.

The Covid-19 pandemic took a terrible toll on our Catholic community as well. Chapel activities, including the celebrations of sacraments and liturgies, were shut down for more than a year and we have not yet fully rebounded. Compared to the days prior to the pandemic, our Mass attendance has dwindled by 60%. Compounded by the distressing clergy sexual abuse scandal, the Catholic community at Fort Belvoir is a shadow of the vibrant environment I encountered upon my arrival back in 1990. Those who have persevered, including retirees, and active-duty families, exhibit strong faith and loyalty. Nonetheless, it is evident that our sense of community is not as robust as it once was, due to the enduring impact of these challenging circumstances. It will be interesting to see what the future holds for the observance of religion on military installations. The Catholic church is particularly vulnerable because of the shortage of Catholic clergy in general and in particular the shortage of Catholic military chaplains. As a part-time contract chaplain, I have filled a gap, but as I age, I wonder who will replace me and how we can continue to provide adequate clergy service to the good people of the Catholic community at Fort Belvoir. This leads to a further discussion about the future of ministry in the Catholic Church; married clergy, the ordination of women to the diaconate and priesthood, and the education and training of lay Catholics to take on professional leadership roles.

During my initial years at Carroll, I also helped my friend, Mike Kelley, who had by then become pastor at St. Martin Catholic Church. In the beginning, I guided the RCIA (Rite of

Christian Initiation for Adults) and assisted with Sunday and weekday Masses. I soon fell in love with the people of St. Martin's. The parish was predominantly African American and I felt very much at home and accepted. The RCIA at St. Martin's was especially interesting to work with as people were coming to learn about Catholicism and becoming Catholics. Father Kelley was taking charge of the parish and we were finding the kind of spirit that we had both experienced in our days together at St. Augustine. With my responsibilities at the high school and more demands being made of my time at Fort Belvoir, I had to gradually pull away from St. Martin's, but to this day whenever I go back to help with Masses, I feel the same sense of welcome and love that makes St. Martin's such a unique Catholic parish. Recently, at my encouragement, Carroll hired the music director at the parish, Nova Payton, to lead the music and drama department. I baptized Nova as an infant at St. Augustine and watched her grow to adulthood. Today she is a Helen Hayes Award-winning actor and singer who appears regularly on local stages and in many other major cities in the US, Canada, Europe, and Japan.

CHAPTER 9
RETIREMENT

"If your love is clothed in . . . patience, understanding, tolerance, and sincerity, . . .

you are treading the same path that Jesus trod and

slowly making his immortal dream – the Reign of unconditional love – a reality."

(Leonardo Boff, *The Following of Jesus*)

In December of 1961, while home for Christmas from college, I attended a Christmas party for Washington seminarians at the old Mackin Catholic High School. At the party, I met Mike Bryant for the first time. He was in the same seminary year as me but attended St. Mary's College in Kentucky. We introduced ourselves, became friends, and later attended Mount Saint Mary's Seminary together. In 1969, we were ordained as priests. A few years after ordination we both ended up working with the same priest, Monsignor Ralph Kuehner. Mike was the associate pastor at Our Lady of Victory where Ralph was the pastor and I was the Assistant Director of the Office of Social Development, where Ralph was the director. Interestingly we were not only colleagues but over the years the three of us became good friends. Mike and I are now best friends.

When my aunt Joan passed away, she left me and three cousins her home in Cambridge. I asked Mike if he would be interested in joining me to buy out the interests of my three cousins. He agreed, and in 1985, we bought the home in Cambridge for $22,000. The house was very small and needed a lot of work; it was located in a rural area across from a mobile home park near the Cambridge airport, not exactly a prime location. We fixed it up, initially intending to use it as a vacation home. However, the 2-hour drive between Washington and Cambridge proved challenging, especially with our limited time off. So, after repairing the house, we rented it out to various tenants for about 15 years and eventually sold it for $44,000. With the proceeds, we bought a two-bedroom, one-bath townhouse in Fairfax Village in Southeast Washington, just around the corner from Mike's childhood home.

Both of us decided that when retirement came, we didn't want to live in rectories. While I made good friends among the priests I lived and worked with during my career, rectories were difficult places to live. The offices were usually located in the rectories, and it often felt like I was working all the time. Rectory living was part of an old model of priesthood, with housekeepers and secretaries attending to the priests' needs, creating an expectation that we would be available all the time. The first rectory I lived in had two full-time maids who prepared three meals every day, did our laundry, made our beds, and cleaned our rooms. We had a parish secretary who worked from 4:00 p.m. to 10:00 p.m. every evening. All our housekeeping and secretarial needs were met, but the price we paid was to be always on call and available for everyone who knocked on the door or rang the phone. By the way, my salary for the first couple of years in ministry was $125 per month. My car payment was $72 per month. I spent about $15 per month on gas and insurance and I gave the rest away in tithing and donations.

Mike and I had numerous conversations over the years about this lifestyle, and we both agreed that we didn't want to continue living that way after retirement. We both wanted to maintain our independence in the community and step away from the day-to-day expectations of parish life. For a few years, we shared the house in Fairfax Village, using it for days off, holidays, and vacations. When my mother passed away in 1996, leaving me a little money, and with some equity in the townhouse, I asked Mike to buy out my share. This allowed me to purchase a one-bedroom condo in Rock Creek Gardens in Silver Spring in 2000. Again, I used the condo on weekends, holidays, and days off while keeping my apartment at Carroll until I retired from full-time ministry in 2014. Once I retired, I relinquished my apartment at the high school and moved to Silver Spring full-time.

During the initial years of retirement, I continued to spend two or three days a week at the school for about 5 hours a day, and I also engaged in pastoral work at Fort Belvoir on weekends. I wanted to use my retirement time for increased prayer, reading, and quality time with family and friends. I sought to gradually distance myself from the day-to-day challenges of fundraising and pastoral work. In the process, however, the demands on my time were still existent. Additionally, I was grappling with the notion of aging, wishing I could be 55 instead of 75. As had in the past when feeling overwhelmed or experiencing situational depression, I sought the hope of a therapist. With his assistance, I recognized that my joy in life was within my control. I also understood that being a priest meant people had certain expectations of me that I couldn't disregard. Over the centuries, Catholics have come to believe that once a priest, always a priest, leading to the anticipation that we will always be available for people's spiritual needs.

My retirement has been wonderful and I have no regrets about retiring when I did, at the age of 70. With prayer and guidance, I have reached a point where I continue to contribute to the high school and engage in pastoral work with enthusiasm and goodwill. At the same time, I enjoy not having to go into an office or be constantly on call. I assist at local parishes with Masses and confessions, continue to hear confessions, and offer Mass every Wednesday at Fort Belvoir and once a month on Sunday services. I also assist the contract chaplain for the Navy at Arlington National Cemetery with burials once or twice a week.

I made a lot of new friends in retirement, around where I live, and especially at the Daily Dish Restaurant in the Rock Creek Shopping Center, directly across from where I live. As long as I can manage three steps into my apartment and cross the street I will stay in my condo. There are three restaurants, a market, cleaners, and a gym all in the shopping center, so life in Silver Spring is very convenient. I also have access to the Montgomery County Ride On bus which gives me easy access to downtown Silver Spring, Bethesda, and Chevy Chase. It's a great location and I know many people in my condo complex and in the neighborhood.

As I write this memoir, at the age of 80, I am content to be alive and relatively healthy. Last year, while reading a book on world religions written by Karen Armstrong with my spirituality group, I came across the Five Remembrances of Foundational Buddhism:

1. I am of the nature to grow old. There is no way to escape growing old.
2. I am of the nature to have ill health. There is no way to escape having ill health.
3. I am of the nature to die. There is no way to escape death.
4. All that is dear to me and everyone I love is of the nature to change. There is no way to escape being separated from them.
5. My actions are my only true belongings. I cannot escape the consequences of my actions. My actions are the ground upon which I stand.

I copied these remembrances and taped them inside my medicine cabinet where I reference them every morning as I brush my teeth. They serve as reminders that life is fragile and the people in my life are blessings, but their presence and love are not guaranteed.

On July 12, 2022, NASA revealed the first images captured by the James Webb Space Telescope to mass audiences. Scientists tell us that the universe is 13.8 billion years old and the Webb telescope can look back 13.7 billion years, almost to the beginning of existence, nearly to the Big Bang. As I observe the stunning images of light, fire, and stars sparkling, exploding, and expanding, I am reminded of the words of the psalmist (somewhat rephrased below):

> "O Lord our God, how awesome is your name through all the earth! ..... When I see your heavens, the work of your fingers, the moon, and the stars that you set in place – who am I that you are mindful of me, a son of man that you care for me? You have made me little less than the angels, crowned me with glory and honor . . . O Lord our God, how awesome is your name through all the earth." (Psalm 8)

A few years ago, I heard Jane Goodall, the famous primatologist, interviewed by Terry Gross on NPR. Terry asked her, if I remember correctly, about her religious beliefs. Jane responded, "I'm a scientist; I believe in the Big Bang. However, I also believe in what was before the Big Bang."

At this age of my life, I look back with wonder and gratitude. I wonder at how I came to this place in the universe and I am so very grateful for my faith in a loving and merciful God. One of the Webb scientists commented recently, "Light is eternal." To say light is eternal means that it has no beginning and no end. Different people have different names: light, energy, love, and God, but whatever we call the mystery of the universe we know it to be creative and purposeful.

When I pray my rosary every night as I fall asleep (my mother told me if I pray the rosary when I go to bed and fall asleep, the angels will finish it) I begin with the Apostles Creed: *I believe in God, the Father . . . I believe in Jesus Christ . . . I believe in the Holy Spirit.* I believe!!! And I am so grateful for my faith and my parents, my brother and sister, their families, my aunts and uncles, all the priests, sisters, and especially all the good Catholic people I have known over the years who have given me and nurtured my faith. I am also grateful that I have come to that place in life where I can recognize and value people of other religious traditions, and even those who have no expressed religion or belief. I prefer to see goodness and kindness working in everyone. Of course, I am not so naive as to believe that there isn't evil in the world and that in all of us, there is a shadow side, or that all of us are capable of doing wrong, but I do believe that as Genesis reminds us: "God saw all that he had made, and it was very good."

I look back on my years as a priest and give thanks to God who guided my path and brought me to this moment. I have some regrets, of course. First, I regret my own personal failures and am sorry for anyone I hurt along the way. I also regret that the institutional Church has not always embraced and continued the vision of the Second Vatican Council. The Holy Spirit has raised up Pope Francis and he renews my hope that the Catholic hierarchy will eventually catch up with the Catholic people who I believe are far ahead on the important issues of our day and how our faith must respond. I look forward to the day that we will have married clergy and when we will ordain women as deacons and priests. I imagine a time when we will acknowledge the many people who are non-traditional in their sexual preferences and lifestyles.

My hope is that our Church will produce and acknowledge men and women prophets who can look beyond ideology and politics and work against the great social evils: racism, sexism, nationalism, homophobia, war, violence, hatred, weapons of war, and the abuses of power and wealth. I long for the day when we will acknowledge and work to correct the great disparity of wealth and resources; that people of faith and good-will will work together to bring about God's vision for the world and creation.

I'm grateful that as I near the conclusion of this wonderful life, I can also look back and appreciate all the good people who were part of my life and who loved me and whom I loved. I have been truly blessed, beginning with my family, and continuing with good friends, colleagues, and parishioners over 54 years as a priest. In every setting, I have been inspired by so many people of deep faith and goodwill. Even among those who say they do not believe, or those who have given up on the Catholic Church, I see goodness and sincerity. I wish sometimes that they would know Jesus as I know Him, and see the world through his eyes. Saint Paul says he is the "image of the invisible God." I wish for those who do not believe or who have grown weak in faith they would have the "joy" that I have experienced, and for that, I continue to pray.

My path to the priesthood began during the era of Pope John XXIII, whose influence sparked the Second Vatican Council and who initiated the Church's engagement with the contemporary world. Now, as I approach the culmination of my journey, we have Pope Francis, who has revitalized the reform efforts set in motion by Vatican II. Pope Francis stands as a contemporary prophet, radiating an authentic love for Jesus that transcends into a profound concern for both humanity and the world. He possesses a unique dedication to those on the margins of society and a special commitment to our common home, our planet. He serves as a constant source of inspiration, continuing to motivate me to dedicate my remaining years to working towards a new world and for the Kingdom of God.

I would like to end this memoir with one of the two prayers that concluded the Encyclical, "Laudato Si," which Pope Francis issued in 2015. I believe this ecumenical prayer reflects my faith and my vision for the world.

A Prayer for Our Earth

All-powerful God, you are present in the whole universe
and in the smallest of your creatures.
You embrace with your tenderness all that exists.
Pour out upon us the power of your love, that
we may protect life and beauty. Fill us with
peace, that we may live as brothers and sisters,
harming no one.

O God of the poor, help us to rescue the
abandoned and forgotten of this earth, so
precious in your eyes. Bring healing to our lives,
that we may protect the world and not prey on
it, that we may sow beauty, not pollution and
destruction.

Touch the hearts of those who look only for gain at the expense of the poor and the earth. Teach us to discover the worth of each thing, to be filled with awe and contemplation, to recognize that we are profoundly united with every creature as we journey towards your infinite light.

We thank you for being with us each day. Encourage us, we pray, in our struggle for justice, love, and peace. Amen

About the Author

Father John J. Mudd was born on July 2, 1943, in Washington, D.C. He was ordained priest for the Archdiocese of Washington in 1969 and embarked on his priestly journey with his initial assignment at Our Lady Queen of Peace Parish in Southeast Washington. Father Mudd acknowledges the invaluable guidance he received during this period, crediting the parishioners of Queen of Peace for teaching him the essence of priesthood.

In 1973, he assumed the role of Assistant Director of the Archdiocesan Office of Social Development. In this capacity, Father Mudd played a pivotal role in developing educational materials and mobilizing churches to engage with urban and social justice matters.

In 1977, he took on the position of Associate Pastor at Saint Augustine Church in Northwest Washington, and from 1981 to 1990, he served as the Pastor of the church. Saint Augustine holds historical significance as the oldest African American parish in the Archdiocese of Washington and one of the earliest African American Catholic Churches in the nation.

During his first two decades as a priest in Washington, Father Mudd witnessed the closure of over 15 Catholic secondary schools, primarily those with predominantly African American student populations. In response to this challenge, in 1990, he voluntarily took on the role of Director of Development for the sole remaining African American Catholic high school at the time owned and operated by the Archdiocese.

From its humble beginnings, where it raised $108,000 in its inaugural year, Father Mudd successfully cultivated a robust network of individual, corporate, and foundation supporters for Archbishop Carroll High School. This network now contributes almost $2 million annually towards the school's operations, scholarships, and tuition assistance.

While Father Mudd officially retired from full-time active ministry in the Archdiocese of Washington in 2013, his commitment to pastoral service remains unwavering. He continues to provide spiritual guidance to the Catholic Community at Fort Belvoir and the Navy Yard, and he also assists with funerals at Arlington National Cemetery. Additionally, he continues to lend his support to fundraising efforts at Archbishop Carroll High School.

Made in the USA
Middletown, DE
10 December 2023

45148227R00053